D0201302

SEVEN SIGNS OF THE END TIMES

MARK HITCHCOCK

Multnomah® Publishers

SEVEN SIGNS OF THE END TIMES
published by Multnomah Publishers
A division of Random House, Inc.
© 2002 by Mark Hitchcock

International Standard Book Number: 1-59052-129-3

Cover design by Kirk DouPonce UDG/DesignWorks
Cover images by Corbis, Photodisc, and Photospin

Unless otherwise indicated, Scripture quotations are from:
New American Standard Bible © 1960, 1977, 1995 by the Lockman
Foundation. Used by permission.

Other Scripture quotations are from:
Holy Bible, New Living Translation (NLT) © 1996. Used by permission of
Tyndale House Publishers, Inc. All rights reserved.
The Holy Bible, King James Version (KJV)
The Holy Bible, New International Version (NIV) © 1973, 1984 by
International Bible Society, used by permission
of Zondervan Publishing House

Multnomah is a trademark of Multnomah Publishers
and is registered in the U.S. Patent and Trademark Office.
The colophon is a trademark of Multnomah Publishers.

Printed in the United States of America

ALL RIGHTS RESERVED
No part of this publication may be reproduced, stored in
a retrieval system, or transmitted, in any form or by any means—
electronic, mechanical, photocopying, recording, or otherwise—
without prior written permission.

For information:
MULTNOMAH PUBLISHERS
12265 ORACLE BOULEVARD, SUITE 200 · COLORADO SPRINGS, CO 80921
Library of Congress Cataloging-in-Publication Data
Hitchcock, Mark.
    Seven signs of the end times / by Mark Hitchcock.
        p. cm.
Includes bibliographical references.
    ISBN 1-59052-129-3 (pbk.)
    1. End of the world. I. Title.
    BT877 .H58 2003
    236' .9--dc21   2002153767

06 07 08 09 10—10 9 8 7 6 5 4 3 2

DEDICATION

To Bob and Marcine Gray

the best in-laws a man could ever have.

CONTENTS

THE AGE OF APOCALYPSE

I'm excited about this fifth book in the End Times Answers series! Incredible events are transpiring in our world that cause even the most hardened skeptics to wonder if we are getting near "closing time." No wonder interest in Bible prophecy is at an all-time high.

Consider these facts. According to a *Time*/CNN poll, since the attacks of September 11, 2001, 35 percent of Americans are paying more attention now to how the news might relate to the end of the world. Seventeen percent believe that the end of the world will happen in their lifetime, and 59 percent believe that the prophecies of the Book of Revelation will come true.[1] More than ever before people are looking at world events with prophetic eyes.

On the other hand, since Jesus returned to heaven with the promise that He would someday come back, nearly every generation has interpreted Bible prophecy in light of its own historical experience. And, every previous generation that thought it was living in the end times was wrong.

So why should we even try to discern the signs of the times? Won't we fall into the same category? Why even write a book about the signs of the times?

I believe that's a legitimate question.

This book is based on four very simple, yet important, conclusions. *First,* the Bible gives a detailed blueprint of the global scene at the end of the age. Many general trends and specific events are clearly marked out. *Second,* many current circumstances bear a striking similarity to the conditions in the end times predicted in the Bible. *Third,* many events in our world now have an almost immediate, worldwide effect. Things happen quickly and their impact is accelerated exponentially, even compared to the events of just fifty years ago. *Fourth,* each person must decide for himself whether he believes we are living in the last days.

No single event leads me to conclude that the end could be very near. Rather, it's the cumulative effect, the convergence of so many more signs than ever before, that causes me to pause and consider. Today we are witnessing an unparalleled correspondence between the trend of world events and Bible prophecy. People from all walks of life and religious backgrounds are asking the same questions. Could the end be near? Is the world well down the road toward Armageddon? What are the additional signs that we should be looking for?

The purpose of this book is to answer these questions. With that objective in mind, I have gathered what I believe are seven of the most striking signs that point to the end. This isn't to say that no other signs of the times exist. Or that some of the others aren't important as well.

But I believe that these are the most notable ones that strikingly foreshadow what the Bible predicts in the final years of this age.

According to the *Time*/CNN poll I mentioned above, 35 percent of Americans "are paying more attention now to how the news might relate to the end of the world." But many of them may not know exactly what they are looking for. In this book I have tried to bring together, in one concise resource, the key trends and developments that seem to be setting the stage for the end times. I have clearly identified seven key things you need to be watching and paying attention to that relate to the end of the age.

In this book, as in the others in this series, I am going to assume that you, the reader, have at least a basic knowledge of a few key events in the end times. Nonetheless, to make sure you understand these events at the outset, let's do a brief review and define a few key terms that you will see sprinkled throughout these pages.

THE RAPTURE OF THE CHURCH TO HEAVEN

This next event on God's prophetic timetable will occur when all who have personally trusted in Jesus Christ as their Savior, the living and the dead, will be caught up to meet the Lord in the air. They will go with Him back up to heaven, then return with Him to earth at least seven years later at His second coming (see John 14:1–3; 1 Corinthians 15:50–58; 1 Thessalonians 4:13–18).

THE SEVEN-YEAR TRIBULATION PERIOD

The Tribulation dominates the final seven years of this age. It will begin with a peace treaty between Israel and Antichrist, and will end with the second coming of

Christ back to earth. During this time the Lord will pour out His wrath upon the earth in successive waves of judgment. But the Lord will also pour out His grace by saving millions of people during this time (see Revelation 6–19).

THE THREE-AND-A-HALF-YEAR WORLD EMPIRE OF ANTICHRIST

During the last half of the Tribulation, Antichrist will rule the world politically, economically, and religiously. The entire world will give allegiance to him or suffer persecution and death (see Revelation 13:1–18).

THE CAMPAIGN OF ARMAGEDDON

The campaign, or war, of Armageddon is the final event of the Great Tribulation when all the armies of the earth gather to come against Israel and attempt once and for all to eradicate the Jewish people (Read Revelation 14:19-20; 16:12-16; 19:19-21).

THE SECOND COMING OF CHRIST TO EARTH

The climactic event of human history is the literal, physical, visible, glorious return of Jesus Christ to planet earth. He will destroy the armies of the world gathered in Israel and set up His kingdom on earth, which will last for 1,000 years (Revelation 20:1–3).

God's Blueprint for the End Times

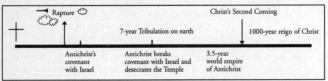

My sincere prayer is that God will use this book to help you better understand how current events seem to be setting the stage for the final drama of the ages. I also pray that it will help make you ready to meet the Lord when He appears.

Maranatha
"Our Lord, Come!"
Mark Hitchcock

HOMECOMING: THE RETURN OF THE JEWISH PEOPLE TO ISRAEL

I have been asked hundreds of questions about Bible prophecy and the end times in the last ten years. Most of the time I am able to give at least some answer to each question, but sometimes I simply have to say, "I don't know."

However, when people ask me, as they frequently do, what I believe is the number one, most important sign of the end times, I respond confidently and without hesitation.

Israel. The modern state of Israel. The return of the Jewish people to Israel. This singular event is a prophetic watershed.

The most prophesied event in end-time passages in

the Bible is the return of the Jewish people to their promised land. The Bible predicts over and over again that the Jews must be back in their homeland for the events of the end times to unfold (see Jeremiah 30:1–3; Ezekiel 34:11–24; Zechariah 10:6–10).

Simply stated, almost all the key events of the end times hinge in one way or another on the existence of the nation of Israel. Israel is the battleground for all the great end-time conflicts and wars described in the Bible.

THE REGATHERING

To properly understand the end-time homecoming, or regathering, of the Jews to their promised land, we need to keep three major points in mind.

First, the Bible predicts that Israel will experience two worldwide, end-time regatherings to the Promised Land.

According to Scripture, Israel will experience two (and only two) international, worldwide returns from exile. The first worldwide regathering will be a return in unbelief in preparation for the judgment of the Tribulation. The second worldwide regathering will be a return in faith at the end of the Tribulation, in preparation for the

14

blessing of the Millennium (one-thousand-year reign) of Christ.[2]

Several Old Testament passages highlight a return of the Jews in spiritual unbelief as a prelude to the discipline of the tribulation period (see Ezekiel 22:17–22; Zephaniah 2:1–2). One especially important passage dealing with Israel's two regatherings is Isaiah 11:11–12.

> Then it will happen on that day that the Lord will again recover the second time with His hand the remnant of His people, who will remain, from Assyria, Egypt, Pathros, Cush, Elam, Shinar, Hamath, and from the islands of the sea. And He will lift up a standard for the nations and assemble the banished ones of Israel, and will gather the dispersed of Judah from the four corners of the earth.

The regathering in the preceding passage clearly refers to the final worldwide regathering of Israel in faith at the climax of the Tribulation, in preparation for the blessing of the millennial kingdom. Isaiah specifically says that this final regathering is the second one. The obvious question then becomes, "When did the first one occur?" Some maintain that the first return was the Babylonian return from exile that began in about 536 B.C. However, this return was not worldwide as described in Isaiah 11.[3]

The only reasonable conclusion then is that the first international regathering must be the one in preparation for the Tribulation. It must be a pretribulational regathering of Israel.

The following chart provides a quick visual comparison and contrast between Israel's two great regatherings.[4]

THE PRESENT (First) Regathering	THE PERMANENT (Second) Regathering
Worldwide	Worldwide
Return to part of the Land	Return to all the Land
Return in unbelief	Return in faith
Restored to the Land only	Restored to the Land and the Lord
Man's work (secular)	God's work (spiritual)
Sets the stage for the Tribulation (discipline)	Sets the stage for the Millennium (blessing)

Since Israel will experience only two worldwide

returns from exile, the present worldwide return of Jews to Israel must be in preparation for the fulfillment of the first international regathering of Israel.

Second, the Bible predicts that Israel's initial regathering will occur in phases, or stages.

In A.D. 70 the land of Israel, the city of Jerusalem, and the Jewish temple were crushed under the heel of Roman domination. Since that time, the Jews have been scattered all over the world.

God's warning of worldwide exile in Deuteronomy 28:64–66 has been literally, graphically fulfilled in the last 1900 years.

> Moreover, the LORD will scatter you among all peoples, from one end of the earth to the other end of the earth…. Among those nations you shall find no rest, and there will be no resting place for the sole of your foot; but there the LORD will give you a trembling heart, failing of eyes, and despair of soul. So your life shall hang in doubt before you; and you will be in dread night and day, and shall have no assurance of your life.

But as we have seen, the Bible predicts that Israel will be regathered to the land in the end times. Scripture further indicates that this regathering will occur in stages. It is portrayed as a process, for it should take some time for the returning exiles to regather and resettle the Land.

In the famous "valley of dry bones" vision of Ezekiel 37:1–14, the bones symbolize the nation of Israel coming back together in the end times. In that passage, Ezekiel sees a graveyard vision illustrating the national return, restoration, and regeneration of "the whole house of Israel" (37:11). Israel is first restored physically. The physical restoration is pictured by the coming together of bones, sinew, and skin. An army of skeletons comes together bone by bone, then each one is covered by tendons, flesh, and skin to become a complete body. Piece by piece. But the army is still made up of lifeless corpses (see 37:8).

Then, Ezekiel witnesses Israel's spiritual regeneration when the breath of the Spirit breathes spiritual life into the dead nation (see 37:9). Of course, this spiritual regeneration won't occur until the Messiah returns.

But I believe the process of physical regathering to the Land has begun. Preparations for the first worldwide regathering of Israel have been going on now for about

130 years. A pile of bones is beginning to come together and take shape in the land of Israel.

Let's consider what has happened so far.

The modern return to Israel began as early as 1871, when a few Jews began to trickle back into the land. By 1882, about 25,000 Jews had settled there. At the First Zionist Congress in 1897, led by Theodore Herzl, the goal of reclaiming the land for the Jewish people was officially adopted. But the regathering was very slow. By 1914, the number of Jews in the land was only 85,000.

During World War I, the British sought support from the Jews for the war effort. In return, the British foreign secretary, Arthur J. Balfour, issued what has since become known as the Balfour Declaration on November 2, 1917. This declaration was contained in a letter from Balfour to Lord Rothschild, who was a wealthy Jewish entrepreneur. In that letter, Secretary Balfour gave approval to the Jewish goal of reclamation. "His Majesty's Government views with favor the establishment in Palestine of a national home for the Jewish people...."

However, because the British desired to maintain friendly relations with the Arabs, little was done to pursue the goals of the Balfour Declaration. Nevertheless, it stirred Jewish hopes for the establishment of a homeland in the Holy Land and encouraged more Jews to return. By 1939, when World War II broke out, about 450,000 Jews had managed to return.

The Second World War and Nazi Germany's heinous, despicable treatment of the Jewish people created worldwide sympathy and a favorable environment for the Jewish people. Hitler's atrocities actually provided the greatest momentum for the establishment of a national homeland for the Jews. The United Nations soon approved a national homeland for the Jews, and British control of the land ended on May 14, 1948. The new nation was given five thousand square miles of territory. At that time it was populated by 650,000 Jews and several hundred thousand Arabs.

Since those days, further waves of immigrants have poured into Israel from all over the world, most notably from Ethiopia and the Soviet Union. By the year 2001, 38 percent of the 13.2 million Jews in the world were back in the land of Israel. To put this in perspective, in 1948 only 6 percent of the Jews in the world were in Israel. Current projections indicate that by the year 2030 half of the Jews in the world will be back in the land of Israel.

Prophetically, the process and preparations over the

last 130 years are staggering. For the first time in two thousand years, the Jews are truly returning to their land.

Third, the regathering of Israel will set the stage for the events of the end times.

The Bible predicts that Israel must be partially regathered to her land for the events of the end times to unfold. End-time prophecy in Scripture is built upon the assumption that Israel will be regathered to her land and functioning as a nation.

The clearest passage on this subject is Daniel 9:27. "And he [Antichrist] will make a firm covenant with the many for one week [one week of years, or seven years]."

According to this verse, the seven-year tribulation period begins with the signing of a covenant between Antichrist and the leaders of Israel. Obviously, the signing of this treaty presupposes the presence of a Jewish leadership in a Jewish nation. This Jewish state must exist before a treaty can be signed.[5]

The logic goes like this. The Tribulation can't begin until the seven-year covenant is signed. The covenant can't be signed until a Jewish state exists. Therefore, a Jewish state must exist before the Tribulation.

I believe the main purpose for the first regathering of

Israel is for the Jews to be present in the land to make the peace pact with Antichrist that is described in Daniel 9:27. This is the event that begins the final seven-year tribulation period. It appears to me that the present regathering of the Jews to their homeland is setting the stage for the fulfillment of their return in unbelief, which will make possible the event that triggers the Tribulation. The Jewish people are organized into a political state, thus making the peace covenant of Daniel 9:27, and the beginning of the Tribulation, possible for the first time since A.D. 70.[6]

This regathering is also paving the way for the final discipline of Israel by God, in the Great Tribulation. God will use this time of unparalleled horror to bring many of the Jewish people to faith in the Lord Jesus as the Messiah of God, who died for their sins and rose again on the third day (see Zechariah 12:10).

During the tribulation period the Jewish people will be scattered over the face of the earth for the final time. The Antichrist will mercilessly persecute them, many will be killed, and many more will flee for their lives (see Daniel 7:25; Matthew 24:15–21). At the end of the tribulation period, Jesus Christ will return from heaven to slay the Antichrist and his armies that have gathered in Israel for the final showdown. Then, the Jewish people will be regathered to the land of Israel from all over the world, for the second and final time, to rule and reign with their Messiah for one thousand years. Finally, all the prophecies about Israel's total possession and blessing in the land will be fulfilled.

LIGHTING THE FUSE

Israel is the powder keg fuse for the final world conflict. Nothing can happen until Israel is back in her land. It all hangs on Israel. The Tribulation can't even start until Israel is back in the land and willing to make peace with the Antichrist. For the first time in almost two thousand years, the fuse is moving into position.

Israel is a nation. Millions of Jews are back in the land. And that's the number one sign of the end times.

WELCOME HOME

Every visitor to modern Israel who enters by plane comes in the same way. You have to go through passport control at the Ben Gurion Airport in Tel Aviv. Millions of people have come and gone through that airport, but most never even notice the big "welcome" sign at the airport.

Randall Price, who is an expert on Israel and Bible

prophecy, provides a powerful description of this welcome sign and its significance.

> Once they have passed through passport control and are about to exit, they are greeted by a huge and colorful tapestry welcoming them to the Land. On it is depicted masses of people streaming into the gates of the City of Jerusalem. On the tapestry, in Hebrew, is a prophetic text from Jeremiah that speaks about the ingathering of the exiles: "So there is hope for your future," declares the Lord. "Your children will return to their own land" (Jeremiah 31:17, NIV). Whether or not the incoming Jewish people can yet read the words, the lesson is understood, for they who are coming home are part of God's present purpose in regathering His people for the fulfillment of His promise.[7]

The number one sign of the end times is the return of the Jewish people to their homeland from worldwide exile.

JERUSALEM: GROUND ZERO FOR THE END TIMES

Since the terrible events of September 11 we have all heard a great deal about "ground zero." Ground zero is the place where the twin towers came crashing down in New York City. The horrible sight of ruin, rubble, and twisted, smoldering wreckage is a scene forever etched in our minds. It's the place where so many lives were tragically taken. It's also a place where many lives were heroically offered up by firemen, police officers, and other rescue workers. That place has become ground zero in the war against terror and for the patriotic unity of our nation.

The Bible says that ground zero for the end times will not be New York City, London, Paris, Tokyo, or Rome. It will be the city of Jerusalem. This city in the tiny nation of Israel (the size of New Jersey) will be the focus of the entire world at the end of the age.

The importance of Jerusalem in God's program is evident from a quick survey of the Bible. A total of 802 verses in the Bible speak of Jerusalem (660 in the Old Testament and 142 in the New). Of these, 489 were prophetic at the time they were given.

On ancient maps, Jerusalem was located at the center of the map. This signified that it was the geographic focal point of man's activity.

Jerusalem is still the city at the center today. Thomas Ice and Timothy Demy observe: "Located at 31 degrees 47 minutes north latitude, 35 degrees 13 minutes east longitude, Jerusalem no longer occupies the center of the cartographer's maps and efforts. It does, however, remain at the center of biblical prophecy. The dynamic story of this glorious city continues today. History proclaims its past. Headlines proclaim its present. Prophecy proclaims its future."[8]

You can open the newspaper every day and find some mention of Jerusalem. The headlines are proclaiming its present. But what is the future for Jerusalem?

JERUSALEM: FUTURE TENSE

Writing in about 500 B.C., the Jewish prophet Zechariah prophesied events that were far distant from his own day. In Zechariah 9–14, the prophet recorded two great burdens, or oracles (prophecies), detailing events surrounding the first and second coming of Israel's Messiah.

Chapters 9–11 contain prophecies of the first coming of Messiah and His rejection. These prophecies, focused on the city of Jerusalem, were literally fulfilled.

Rejoice greatly, O daughter of Zion! Shout in triumph, O daughter of Jerusalem! Behold, your king is coming to you; He is just and endowed with salvation, humble, and mounted on a donkey, even on a colt, the foal of a donkey. (Zechariah 9:9)

I said to them, "If it is good in your sight, give me my wages; but if not, never mind!" So they weighed out thirty shekels of silver as my wages. Then the LORD said to me, "Throw it to the potter, that magnificent price at which I was valued by them." So I took the thirty shekels of silver and threw them to the potter in the house of the LORD. (Zechariah 11:12–13)

Zechariah's second message, in chapters 12–14, centers on Messiah's second coming and acceptance. And just as with Jesus' first coming, ground zero for the events surrounding His second coming is the city of Jerusalem.

> Behold, I am going to make Jerusalem a cup that causes reeling to all the peoples around; and when the siege is against Jerusalem, it will also be against Judah. It will come about in that day that I will make Jerusalem a heavy stone for all the peoples; all who lift it will be severely injured. And all the nations of the earth will be gathered against it. (Zechariah 12:2–3)

The Bible says that in the end times, Israel and Jerusalem will dominate the attention of the entire world in a negative way. Jerusalem will be at the center of international controversy and conflict. The nations will become intoxicated with the desire to possess the city. They will seek to internationalize it and control its future. But Zechariah says that all who try to drink of it will find calamity. Everyone who attempts to carry off or remove Jerusalem for their own purposes will quickly discover that she is a heavy, jagged stone that will cut them to pieces.

Therefore, as the end times draw near, we should expect to see mounting tension and conflict between Israel and the surrounding nations. We should also anticipate that Jerusalem will be the center of this conflict as Israel's neighbors try to wrench control of the city away from the Jewish people.

This is precisely what we see unfolding today. The issue in all the peace talks is Jerusalem. The peace process constantly bogs down on the issue of Jerusalem and the Temple Mount.

Remember a few years ago when the saying was, "It's the economy, stupid"? Well, in current international politics we could say, "It's Jerusalem, stupid!" The issue is Jerusalem.

But have you ever wondered why? Why is Jerusalem the sticking point? Why is Jerusalem at the center of the storm?

WHY JERUSALEM?

Jerusalem is at the center of the storm today for one simple reason: It's claimed by two world religions (Judaism and Islam) as sacred ground. Jerusalem is the sacred battleground in the ongoing struggle between Jews and Muslims.

For Jews, Jerusalem is the spiritual and emotional heart of their religion. Here's a brief overview of the seven significant events that make Jerusalem so important to Jews.

1. Abraham was called by God to offer Isaac on Mount Moriah. This mountain is currently known as the Temple Mount in Jerusalem (see Genesis 22:2).

2. God chose Jerusalem as the place for the Israelites to worship Him (see Deuteronomy 12:5).

3. King David made Jerusalem the capital city for Israel (see 2 Samuel 5:6–10).

4. David purchased the land on Mount Moriah (see 1 Chronicles 21:18–22:1).

5. David's son Solomon constructed his temple on the site of Mount Moriah (see 2 Chronicles 3:1).

6. After the destruction of the temple by the Babylonians and the seventy-year exile to Babylon, the Jews returned to Jerusalem and

rebuilt the temple there on Mount Moriah.

7. When the second temple was destroyed by the Romans in A.D. 70, the Jews were scattered all over the earth. When they began to return to Israel and became a nation in 1948, guess what city they named as their capital? Jerusalem!

Of course, this action inflamed Muslims all over the Middle East because Jerusalem is an important holy place in Islam. Jerusalem is never mentioned in the Koran, the holy book of Islam. However, according to Islamic tradition, the Temple Mount in Jerusalem is the place from which Muhammad ascended to heaven on his night journey. The famous Dome of the Rock covers the rock where Muhammad allegedly left his footprint as he leaped to heaven. The Al-Aqsa Mosque on the Temple Mount is considered the third holiest site in Islam, behind Mecca and Medina.

Islam also teaches that land conquered in the name of Allah (the Islamic god) remains in his possession forever. Since Israel and Jerusalem were conquered in his name, it is a direct insult and affront to Muslims for these lands to be in Jewish hands. In fact, the visit of Ariel Sharon, the current Prime Minister of Israel, to the Temple Mount is what ignited the Palestinian *intifada* (uprising) that began on September 26, 2000.

And there you have it in a nutshell. That's the problem. Jerusalem is the city at the center, the major sticking point in all the Middle East peace negotiations. What we see today is a fitting prelude to the Bible's prediction of the place of Jerusalem in the end times.

It's amazing that this one small piece of ground could capture so much attention. The only explanation is supernatural. God has sovereignly placed Israel in the eye of the hurricane to fulfill His Word. As we draw closer to the coming of Christ, Jerusalem and the Temple Mount will remain in the world's crosshairs.

THE CITY OF PEACE

One of the great ironies in the Bible is that the word *Jerusalem* means "possession of peace." However, there is not a city in the world that has experienced more conflict than Jerusalem

But the good news is that someday Jerusalem will live up to its name. When will this happen? When Jesus Christ, the Prince of Peace, returns at the end of the

Tribulation to rule and reign. This event is described in Zechariah 14:2, 4.

> For I will gather all the nations against Jerusalem to battle…. In that day His feet will stand on the Mount of Olives, which is in front of Jerusalem on the east; and the Mount of Olives will be split in its middle from east to west by a very large valley, so that half of the mountain will move toward the north and the other half toward the south.

Jesus will return to the Mount of Olives, the hill just east of Jerusalem that overlooks the Temple Mount. From there He will annihilate the armies that have gathered at Armageddon to destroy Jerusalem and wipe out the Jewish people. Jerusalem will be ground zero for Christ's return, retribution, and reign over all the earth.

So what is God telling us? Watch Jerusalem! She is the key.

And what do we see as we look at Jerusalem? It's like looking in a mirror that reflects what the Bible predicts. Today's headlines bear a remarkable correspondence to the Biblical predictions of Jerusalem's place in the end times.

The stage is being set for the events in Zechariah 12–14 to be fulfilled, just as God predicted.

THE REUNITING OF THE ROMAN EMPIRE

I was at the checkout stand of a store recently when the front cover of a weekly tabloid caught my eye. In huge letters the front cover read: NEXT 100 DAYS REVEALED.

Two things instantly struck me. First, this kind of title sells. Why? Because people want to know the future. Plain and simple. People have always had a fascination with the future. And in the troubled, unstable world of today, more than ever, people would love to know what the future holds.

Second, when I saw that cover I was instantly reminded that no human can accurately unveil tomorrow, or even the next hour, let alone the next hundred days. But God can. God says that He alone can tell the future. He offers this as incontrovertible proof that He is the true God.

> For I am God—I alone! I am God, and there is no one else like me. Only I can tell you what is going to happen even before it happens. Everything I plan will come to pass, for I do whatever I wish. (Isaiah 46:9b–10, NLT)

The Jewish prophet Daniel was given a revelation by God that revealed not the next day or even the next one hundred days, but what now has been more than 2,500 years. Of course, Daniel was not given every detail. But he was shown the major flow of world history from his own day, in about 550 B.C., until the second coming of Jesus Christ to earth to rule and reign forever. His incredible prophecy is as relevant today as it was the day it was written.

THE TIMES OF THE GENTILES

Daniel wrote his great prophecy in about 550–530 B.C. He wrote during the seventy-year Jewish exile in Babylon. God knew that His people would have all kinds of questions during this time of divine discipline. *Is God finished with us? Will God be true to his covenant with Abraham and give us the land of Israel forever? Will the kingdom promised to David ever be realized? Will Messiah ever come to rule and reign over the earth?*

In Daniel 2 and 7, God comforted His people and answered their questions by giving them an overview of the course of world history. God wanted them to know that His promises were sure. That He would keep His Word. That the kingdom would come to Israel.

However, God also wanted them to know that the kingdom would not come immediately. Before the King and His kingdom would come, four great world empires would rule over Israel in succession. With the benefit of historical hindsight, we now know that these four empires were Babylon, Medo-Persia, Greece, and Rome.

In Daniel 2, these four empires are pictured as four metals in a great statue. In Daniel 7, they are pictured as four great wild beasts that come out of the Mediterranean Sea. Here are the obvious parallels between Daniel 2 and 7.

WORLD EMPIRE	DANIEL 2	DANIEL 7
Babylon	Head of gold	Lion
Medo-Persia	Chest and arms of silver	Bear
Greece	Belly and thighs of brass	Leopard
Rome	Legs of Iron	Terrible beast

So far, so good.

But in both Daniel 2 and Daniel 7, the fourth empire, Rome, has a unique feature. It's different than the first three world empires in that it appears in two phases. In Daniel 2, the Roman Empire is symbolized by legs of iron and feet (with ten toes) of iron mixed with clay. Likewise, in Daniel 7, the fourth terrible beast that represents the Roman Empire has ten horns on its head. What does this tell us?

It tells us that Rome will live again!

ROME II

The Bible predicts, in Daniel 2 and 7, that the Roman Empire will exist in two phases. The first phase would follow the Greek empire. This occurred when Rome ruled the world from approximately 100 B.C. until A.D. 476.

The second phase of the Roman Empire, according to Daniel, will emerge prior to the coming of Christ to rule and reign over the earth. This second phase will take the form of a coalition, or a confederation, of ten nations (symbolized by the ten toes in Daniel 2 and the ten horns in Daniel 7) that will encompass the same basic geographical territory as the original, or first phase, of the Roman Empire. We know that this phase of the Roman Empire is future, because the Roman Empire never existed in a ten-kingdom form as revealed by Daniel.

In presenting these two phases of the Roman empire, Daniel skips over many centuries, from historical Rome all the way to end-time prophecy. This kind of "prophetic skip" is consistent with much Old Testament prophecy. As prophecy expert John Walvoord says:

> This view is consistent with a principle of Old Testament, namely, that prophecy from the Old Testament will frequently describe, in much detail, events that are prophetically fulfilled up

to the first coming of Christ, including the first coming, but then skip from that almost immediately into end-time prophecy, describing the Great Tribulation and the events that climax it.[9]

The final, end-time, ten-nation (or ten-kingdom) form of the Roman Empire is pictured in Daniel 2 as the ten toes on the great metallic image and in Daniel 7 as ten horns on the fourth or terrible beast. Notice again the parallels between Daniel 2 and 7, especially in the final phase of the Roman Empire.

WORLD EMPIRE	DANIEL 2	DANIEL 7
Babylon	Head of gold	Lion
Medo-Persia	Chest and arms of silver	Bear
Greece	Belly and thighs of brass	Leopard
Rome (historical)	Legs of iron	Terrible beast
Rome (future)	Ten toes	Ten horns

A.D. 476–TODAY

The Roman Empire was not destroyed in the same way that the empires preceding it were. It was not replaced by another world empire. Instead, in A.D. 476 the heart of the empire was conquered and divided up into pieces that eventually became the nations of Europe. Since that time there have been numerous attempts to bring the fractured empire back together again. Napoleon tried. Hitler tried. But all attempts have failed.

Two events in the 20th century provided the necessary impetus for the reuniting of Europe, which was the core of the historical Roman Empire. I'm referring to World War I and World War II. For centuries the nations of Europe fought one another again and again. But in the aftermath of World War II, a dramatic change occurred. Instead of building up for the next great armed conflict, as they had done for almost 1,600 years, the nations of Europe decided to come together in a coalition that was originally called the Common Market.

Think about it! For the first time in 1,500 years, the necessary preconditions for a reunited, revived Roman Empire, or the second stage of the Roman empire predicted by Daniel, were in place. John Walvoord notes the prophetic significance of these events.

The situation thus establishes, at least on the surface, a peaceful relationship between these major countries. This is a necessary prelude to the revival of the Roman Empire as prophesied in the Bible.[10]

The reunification began officially in 1957 with the Treaty of Rome. Since then, gradually yet steadily, the nations of Europe have come together one by one. Amazingly, this modern amalgamation of nations has taken only forty-five years.

On the following page is a brief sketch of some of the key events and dates of the recent reuniting of the Roman Empire.

Ten more nations are expected to join in 2004: Hungary, Poland, the Czech Republic, Slovenia, Latvia, Lithuania, Slovakia, Estonia, Malta, and Cyprus. In 2007, Bulgaria and Romania are also expected to join.

PUTTING HUMPTY-DUMPTY BACK TOGETHER AGAIN

The EU today has a 626-member parliament, a parliament building in Strasbourg, France that is built to resemble the Tower of Babel, a presidency that rotates among the member nations every six months, a supreme court, a passport,

Event	Date
The birth of the modern European Union (Treaty of Rome), comprised of six nations: Belgium, Germany, Luxembourg, France, Italy, and the Netherlands (a total of 220 million people).	1957
The EEC (European Economic Community) is formed: Denmark, Ireland, and Great Britain join, bringing 66 million more people.	1973
Greece joins the EEC, becoming the tenth member.	1981
Portugal and Spain join the EEC.	1986
Austria, Finland, and Sweden join the EU, bringing the total population to 362 million among the fifteen members.	1995
The monetary union of the EU, with a currency called the Euro.	January 1, 1999
The Euro currency is officially issued.	January 1, 2002

numerous committees, and one currency that has been approved by twelve of the fifteen member nations and is presently in circulation. It is working toward a unified military and criminal justice system.

What we have seen developing in Europe the last forty-five years looks strikingly similar to what the Bible predicts for the end times. The basic governmental and economic components are in place for one man to come on the scene in the EU and ascend to tremendous power. That man will be the Antichrist; he will rule over the final form of the Roman Empire and ultimately the whole world.

The events we see in Europe today seem to be the prelude to the reunited Roman Empire prophesied by Daniel over 2,500 years ago.

As prophecy scholars Thomas Ice and Timothy Demy aptly conclude:

> One would have to be totally ignorant of developments within the world of our day not to admit that, through the efforts of the European Union, "Humpty-Dumpty" is finally being put back together again. This is occurring, like all of the other needed developments of prophecy, at just the right time to be in place for the coming tribulation period.[11]

THE MIDDLE EAST PEACE PROCESS

W hat is the one issue in our world today that overshadows all others? What is the one problem that has festered in the world's side for decades? What is the one issue that finds its way into the world's newspapers and television news reports every day?

The ongoing hostilities in the Middle East. The Mideast peace process. This one continuing crisis monopolizes world attention.

Have you every wondered why?

Certainly, there are political and humanitarian reasons for the world's interest in this ongoing struggle. But I believe there's more to it than that. The Middle East peace process is another important sign of the times.

It is setting the stage for the final covenant of peace between Antichrist and Israel predicted in the Bible.

FIFTY YEARS OF FIGHTING

The modern peace process in the Middle East really began about ninety years ago. The two main parties in this effort were Emir Feisal, the son of the sharif of Mecca, and Chaim Weizmann, the leader of the Zionist Commision to Palestine who later became the first president of Israel. These men forged an agreement in 1919, but it never really got off the ground because of a lack of French and British support.

The movement toward peace has been plowing uphill now for about fifty years. Since the official foundation of Israel as a nation on May 14, 1948, the world has witnessed one long "peace process" between Israel and her Arab neighbors. But there has been no peace. Only brief periods of no war.

The Arab nations surrounding Israel have been in a declared state of war with Israel since May 14, 1948. Here is a brief sketch of the ongoing hostilities between Israel and her neighbors.

1948–49—Israel fought her very first war. When Israel officially became an independent state on May 14, 1948, she was immediately attacked from all sides by Egypt, Jordan, Iraq, Syria, Lebanon, and Saudi Arabia. When a truce was implemented on January 7, 1949, Israel had expanded her territory from five thousand square miles to eight thousand, including much of the Negev, the huge desert to the south between Israel and Egypt.

1956—Israel fought the Suez War with Egypt. On October 29, 1956, when Egyptian leader Gamal Abdel Nasser nationalized the Suez Canal, Israel invaded the Sinai peninsula and took control. Later, Israel returned the Sinai to Egypt.

1964—The Palestinian Liberation Organization (PLO) was formed for the dual purpose of creating a Palestinian state and destroying Israel.

1967—The famous Six-Day War (June 5–10) occurred. Israel captured the Sinai peninsula from Egypt, the West Bank from Jordan, the Golan Heights from Syria, and seized control of Jerusalem.

1973—Egypt and Syria initiated the Yom Kippur War. At 2:00 P.M. on October 6, 1973, on Israel's most holy day, the Day of Atonement (Yom Kippur), these two nations attacked Israel. After heavy fighting, Israel repelled the invaders.

1982–85—The War with Lebanon. After numerous terrorist incidents, Israel attacked Lebanon on June 5, 1982, to disarm the terrorists who were using Lebanon as a sanctuary. Israeli troops withdrew from Lebanon on May 31, 1985. However, Israel didn't pull all of its troops until May 24, 2000.

1987—The First Palestinian *Intifada* (uprising) began in Gaza. This uprising ended in 1993 with the signing of the Oslo Accords.

2000—The Second Palestinian Intifada began. The Palestinians launched this one in September 2000; it continues today. The Palestinians have done most of their killing via suicide (homicide) bombers.

As you can see, the brief history of modern Israel is a history of war. And futile attempts to grab the phantom of peace.

FIFTY YEARS OF FAILURE

The United States, the Soviet Union, the United Nations, and various European nations have all given the Middle East peace process their best shots…and failed. In the United States, president after president and secretary of state after secretary of state have failed to make any real, lasting headway in stopping the ongoing hostilities between Israel and her neighbors.

The United States was able to broker peace treaties between Israel and her two neighbors, Egypt and Jordan. But both of these nations continue to harbor deep hatred toward Israel and consistently side with other Arab nations on issues involving conflict with Israel. The Oslo Accords, signed on September 13, 1993, on the White House lawn by Yitzhak Rabin and Yasser Arafat, brought great hope. But the second *intifada* that began on September 26, 2000, between Israel and the Palestinians, dashed all those fervent hopes.

We often wonder, *Will there ever be peace in the Middle East?*

IMAGINE

Several years ago, not long after the Beatles split up, John Lennon recorded a song entitled "Imagine." One of the lines in the song says, "Imagine all the people, living life in peace." When I hear that song, I almost want to laugh out loud because I'm reminded that the four members of the Beatles couldn't even live in peace with one another. How did Lennon think the whole world could ever live in peace?

However, the Bible does say that a time of peace, albeit a false, temporary peace, is coming for the world. According to Daniel 9:27, the ultimate false messiah, the coming Antichrist, will broker a seven-year peace deal in the Middle East. "And he will make a firm covenant with the many for one week."

Imagine what the world response will be. Imagine the exhilaration, the excitement, the ecstasy. People will believe that peace has finally come to our war-torn, war-weary world. I remember the excitement in 1993 when the Oslo Accords were signed. It was hailed as a new day in Mideast relations. Hopes were high.

However, we don't actually have to imagine what the world response will be when Antichrist brings his peace program to the Middle East. The Bible tells us clearly how the world will respond. People will believe that peace and safety have finally arrived. It will look like the peace to end all peace has finally arrived. People everywhere will be saying, "All is well; everything is peaceful and secure" (1 Thessalonians 5:3, NLT). Man will believe he has finally achieved his goal of peace on earth.

Of course, man's hopes will be quickly dashed. Antichrist's peace will be a false peace. First Thessalonians 5:3 goes on to say, "When people are saying, 'All is well; everything is peaceful and secure,' then disaster will fall upon them as suddenly as a woman's birth pains begin when her child is about to be born. And there will be no escape" (NLT). The rider on the red horse, the second horseman of the apocalypse, will ride forth to take peace from the earth, and the worldwide bloodbath of the Tribulation will begin (see Revelation 6:3–4).

FROM B.C. TO TV

I don't believe that the ongoing hostilities between Israel and her neighbors, and the unending Middle East peace process are accidents. These events are setting the stage for the final peace process ushered in by Antichrist. As you read the paper each day and listen to the television news reports about the Middle East, remember that the Bible in 550 B.C. predicted that Antichrist would come to power on a platform of peace for Israel. What could be more relevant in our world today?

Current events in the Middle East today point clearly toward the precise scenario outlined in the Bible. It's really amazing when you think about it. We have the privilege of witnessing the developing and unfolding of this sign every day on TV. Events we see today seem to harmonize with what the Bible predicts for the climax of the ages.

This should fill us with a sense of excitement, anticipation, and motivation to faithfully serve our precious

Savior. May God empower and energize us to be pure vessels that He can use as we eagerly await His coming.

"But we do know that when he comes we will be like him, for we will see him as he really is. And all who believe this will keep themselves pure, just as Christ is pure" (1 John 3:2b–3, NLT).

IRAQ, BABYLON, AND THE FINAL MIDDLE EAST CRISIS

Next to the Israeli-Palestinian problem, what is the other chronic thorn in the side of the Middle East? Iraq.

Beginning in 1990 with the attack of Kuwait, Saddam Hussein became public enemy number one of the entire world. Since that time he has done everything he can to put Israel and the West between Iraq and a hard place.

This has led many to ask, "Does the rise of Iraq to world prominence have any significance for the end times? Could the events there over the past decade be a sign of the times?" Of course, the Bible says nothing about the war that occurred in the Gulf in the early '90s. However, the gathering of the nations of the world in the Middle East to prevent further aggression created a scenario that led many to see a climate for prophetic fulfillment.

I believe the prominence of Iraq is another key sign of the times.

But I don't want you to just take my word for it. Let's investigate what the Bible says about Iraq, or Babylon—past and future!

And then let's see how current events seem to be setting the stage for what the Bible predicts.

THE CITY OF MAN

As we have already seen, Jerusalem is the most mentioned city in the pages of the Bible—just over eight hundred times. It is first mentioned in Genesis 14 and last mentioned in Revelation 21. Jerusalem is consistently pictured in the Bible in a positive light. It is the city of God.

What many people may not realize is that the second most mentioned city in the Bible is Babylon—about 290 times. The ancient city is located on the Euphrates River in modern Iraq near the Persian Gulf.

Babylon first appears in Genesis 10–11 and last appears in Revelation 17–18. Throughout the Bible, in contrast to Jerusalem, Babylon is pictured as man's city. It is consistently portrayed as a place of rebellion and pride. It was the first city built after the flood. It was the location of the famous Tower of Babel.

In Genesis 14, both Jerusalem (ancient Salem) and Babylon (ancient Shinar) are mentioned. In this chapter the two cities are in conflict. They are on opposite sides of the fence. Babylon attacks Jerusalem and carries away its citizens, including Abraham's nephew Lot.

From this point on, we have what Charles Dyer, an expert on Babylon, calls "The Tale of Two Cities."[12] It's Jerusalem (God's city) versus Babylon (man's city). The story of these two cities takes us from the beginning to the end. It begins in Genesis and ends in Revelation.

In Revelation 17–18, Babylon is finally destroyed by God. But in Revelation 21, the new Jerusalem comes down out of heaven from God as the capital city of the new heaven and new earth, and the eternal abode of God and His people.

That's how the story ends. Man's city falls, but God's city remains. That's the overview of Babylon, past and future.

With this general blueprint in mind, let's delve into a few of the details the Bible gives us about Babylon's history and destiny.

BABYLON IN HISTORY

Most of the references in the Bible to Babylon concern the Babylonian empire that ruled the world of that day. From 605 to 539 B.C., King Nebuchadnezzar and his successors were the great leaders of this empire. Nebuchadnezzar invaded Judah three times. In the first invasion (605 B.C.), Daniel was taken captive. The second time the Babylonians came, in 597 B.C., they carried Ezekiel away. Finally, in 586 B.C., Nebuchadnezzar's forces came and destroyed the great temple of Solomon in Jerusalem.

Many of the prophets, including Isaiah, Jeremiah, Ezekiel, and Habakkuk, wrote about the Babylonians. This evil empire was the great menacing lion of the sixth century B.C.

The prophets warned Judah to repent or else God would send the Babylonians as an instrument of His discipline. However, once the Babylonians had come and destroyed the temple, the message changed from one of judgment on Judah to one of hope for the future. Part of this message of comfort and hope was that God would repay Babylon for her sin. This message was intended to give God's people comfort, encouragement, and hope.

"FALLEN, FALLEN IS BABYLON THE GREAT!"

The Bible gives a detailed description of the destruction of Babylon in several key passages: Isaiah 13; Isaiah 46–47; and Jeremiah 50–51.

Isaiah 13:1, 4–5 says,

> The oracle concerning Babylon which Isaiah the son of Amoz saw.... A sound of tumult on the mountains, like that of many people! A sound of the uproar of kingdoms, of nations gathered together! The LORD of hosts is mustering the army for battle. They are coming from a far country, from the farthest horizons, the LORD and His instruments of indignation, to destroy the whole land.

In this passage, God clearly announces that Babylon will be destroyed by a host of nations. The questions this raises include, When did or when will this destruction occur? What destruction of Babylon is Isaiah talking about? Was this one that occurred in Isaiah's day? Was he prophesying about the overthrow that occurred in 539 B.C., when Babylon fell to the Medo-Persians? Or, did Isaiah look far down the road to a destruction of Babylon in the end times?

BABYLON IN PROPHECY

The rest of Isaiah 13 provides three important clues to help us answer these questions. First, in Isaiah 13:6, 9 the Lord gives an indication of the time of this event. He says that the destruction will occur in the Day of the Lord.

> Wail, for the day of the LORD is near! It will come as destruction from the Almighty.... Behold, the day of the LORD is coming, cruel, with fury and burning anger, to make the land a desolation; and He will exterminate its sinners from it.

The phrase *the Day of the Lord* occurs nineteen times in the Bible. It refers to any time that God dramatically intervenes in human affairs to bring judgment or blessing. However, in most cases, judgment is what's involved. It's when God comes down to earth to settle accounts with sinful man. This phrase is often used to describe the final Day of the Lord during the Great Tribulation (Joel 2:31; 3:14).

Second, the Lord further narrows down the time. We know that it will occur in the Day of the Lord. But which Day of the Lord? It's clear from the context that this destruction of Babylon will be in the final Day of the Lord during the tribulation period.

Reading a little farther in Isaiah 13, we are grabbed by these words:

> For the stars of heaven and their constellations will not flash forth their light; the sun will be dark when it rises and the moon will not shed its light. Thus I will punish the world for its evil and the wicked for their iniquity; I will also put an end to the arrogance of the proud and abase the haughtiness of the ruthless. I will make mortal man scarcer than pure gold and mankind than the gold of Ophir. Therefore I will make the heavens tremble, and the earth will be shaken from its place at the fury of the LORD of hosts in the day of His burning anger (Isaiah 13:10–13).

Nothing even close to this happened in 539 B.C. when Babylon was captured by the Persians. These cosmic disturbances and supernatural signs in the heavens are described elsewhere in the Bible in conjunction with the second coming of Christ to earth (see Joel 3:14–16; Matthew 24:27–30).

Third, Isaiah 13:19 says that when Babylon is finally destroyed it will be like Sodom and Gomorrah. "And Babylon, the beauty of kingdoms, the glory of the Chaldeans' pride, will be as when God overthrew Sodom and Gomorrah." In other words, Babylon will be totally wiped out. Wiped off the face of the earth.

The question we are forced to ask is, When did this ever happen in the past? It didn't. Nothing like this has ever happened to the city of Babylon in its long and storied history. Even when the Persians under King Cyrus conquered Babylon in 539 B.C., the city wasn't destroyed.

There's only one time in man's history when all this will occur: at the end of the Tribulation in conjunction with the second coming of Jesus Christ.

So what does this mean? It means that if the prophecy concerning Babylon is to be literally fulfilled, then this must be referring to a future destruction of Babylon that has not yet occurred. Babylon must rise again, then be totally wiped out in the final Day of the Lord.

BACK TO BABYLON

The final Old Testament prophecy about Babylon is found in Zechariah 5:5–11. This prophecy also indicates that Babylon will be rebuilt in the end times.

The prophet Zechariah sees a vision of a basket that is full of evil and wickedness, personified as a woman. A heavy lid is put on the basket to keep the evil in check. God doesn't want the wickedness to get out. As Zechariah sees the basket being carried away, he asks a question. "Where are they taking the ephah [basket]?" The answer is given. "To build a temple for her in the land of Shinar [Babylon]; and when it is prepared, she will be set there on her own pedestal."

Zechariah is telling us that wickedness will someday be focused again in the land of Babylon. When the necessary preparations have been made, wickedness will return to the place of its origin—Babylon.

BEAUTY ON THE BEAST

The first mention of Babylon in the Bible is in Genesis 10–11, in connection with a tower built to exalt man's pride and a world ruler named Nimrod. The final mention of Babylon is in Revelation 17–18, where the city of man is symbolized by a seductive harlot riding on the back of the Antichrist, who is symbolized by a wild beast. This connection between Babylon and Antichrist indicates that the two will be closely allied. Babylon will probably be some kind of economic, commercial capital for Antichrist.

Revelation 17–18 prophesies the final destruction of Babylon just before the second coming of Jesus Christ in Revelation 19. So, the final act of God before His Son returns to earth is the destruction of Babylon, man's city.

Babylon Today

We have seen an overview of Babylon's past and future in the pages of God's Word. And we have discovered that the prophecies concerning Babylon's final destruction have never been literally fulfilled. Therefore, I believe that Babylon must be rebuilt in the end times as a center of commercialism, greed, and pride, and must suffer total annihilation at the hand of God.

Now we need to ask, Are there events in Babylon today that point toward the fulfillment of the biblical predictions for that place? Could ancient Babylon on the

Euphrates River actually be rebuilt as a major world economic center?

I believe there are four main factors that indicate that Babylon could quickly become the city described in end-time prophecy.

First, Saddam Hussein, who fancies himself a modern Nebuchadnezzar, has begun restoration and building efforts in ancient Babylon on the Euphrates. While the rebuilding efforts are incomplete, the fact that initial steps have already been taken is incredible.

Second, Iraq sits on at least the second largest known crude oil reserves in the world (estimated at 115 billion barrels compared to Saudi Arabia with 261 billion barrels). However, some believe that Iraq may have as much as 300 billion barrels, or 30 percent, of the known reserves in the world. Just next door, tiny Kuwait has 10 percent of the known oil reserves.

The ouster of Saddam from power, or his acquiescence to the UN demands, will result in a lifting of the sanctions and limitations on Iraqi oil sales. Billions of dollars, euros, and yen will begin to flood into Iraq again. This fact alone makes the rebuilding of Babylon as a major economic center for the Middle East and the world a serious possibility. If Iraq were to successfully annex Kuwait in the future, as they tried to do in 1991, Iraq would control an unbelievable 40 percent of the world's oil reserves.

Third, Iraq has become, and continues to be, the major focal point in the Middle East and Persian Gulf. It's interesting to note that Iraq has seemingly come out of nowhere in the past 10–15 years to play a key role in the world. And yet, knowing what the Bible says about Babylon in the end times, the rise of Iraq shouldn't surprise us. This rise could serve as a perfect prelude for the rebuilding of Babylon in the near future.

Fourth, the name *Babylon* evokes notions of intrigue, mystery, pleasure, and power. In *Webster's New Collegiate Dictionary,* Babylon is defined as "a city devoted to materialism and the pursuit of sensual pleasure."[13] I noticed the other day that one of the recent Rolling Stones tours was entitled Bridges to Babylon.

What better place for Antichrist to locate a major economic center than Babylon? It's in the geographical center of the Persian Gulf area surrounded by rich oil reserves. It's not far from Iraq's borders with Iran, Kuwait, and Saudi Arabia, thus affording a strategic location between these four oil-rich nations. It's the ancient capital of King Nebuchadnezzar. It's the place where Alexander the Great died in 323 B.C., intending to make it his eastern capital.

The symbolism of such a move would be incredible. Antichrist could put his eastern capital there just as Alexander the Great attempted to do, symbolically emphasizing his power over the world economy by controlling the main oil fields of the world.

While we don't know exactly how Babylon will be rebuilt, or what will motivate men to carry out this task, I believe that the Bible says it will occur. And current events seem to indicate that it could be soon.

EYE ON IRAQ

Is the rise of Iraq to world prominence an accident? Is the incredible oil wealth of Iraq just a stroke of good fortune? I don't think so. The resurgence of Iraq, the efforts that have already been made to restore and rebuild Babylon, and the incredible oil wealth that could very likely be available soon for finishing the extravagant rebuilding of the city all point toward the picture the Bible paints for Babylon in the end times.

Charles Dyer notes the significance of the rise of Iraq:

Babylon is pictured as a place that sea captains and merchants are going to. It's a place that controls the world economically with her wealth, that even somehow has a relationship to the Antichrist. The Antichrist has military power, but this economic power exerts control over him.

God put the oil in the ground, God sets the stage of world history, and I believe when the final events are ready, when the final curtain goes up, Babylon's going to be there. It's going to be there as an economic powerhouse. It's not there yet. Saddam Hussein has not made Babylon all that the Bible says it will be, but Saddam Hussein or someone who follows him could make it that in a matter of weeks. All it would take is controlling the oil wealth and then saying, "I'm going to make that place even greater than I've made it so far. It's going to become my capital." And at that point, Babylon is everything the Bible says it would be.[14]

Keep your eye on Iraq in the days ahead. Current events there are another part of the matrix of events in the Middle East that are setting the stage for the coming Middle East crisis predicted in God's Word.

THE NEW GLOBALISM

GATT
NAFTA
WTO
NATO
UN
IMF
WSSD

T he acronyms above look like a kid has been messing around in a bowl of Post Alphabet's. (For those too young to remember, Alphabet's was a kind of cereal that people my age used to eat, which helped us learn the alphabet at the same time—providing we read it before we ate it, of course.)

But the acronym game is anything but child's play.

It's serious business. There are more regional, world, and international organizations today than I can keep up with. New acronyms are sprouting up like weeds in a spring lawn.

The effects of globalism are everywhere. Just think about it. The Kyoto Protocol that was adopted on December 11, 1997 is an attempt to regulate world environmental conditions. A decade ago, before attacking Iraq, the United States felt compelled to make its case before the United Nations to get international approval. Acting without UN approval today is the unpardonable international sin. The UN has become the final arbiter of international conflicts.

I believe the globalism we see developing today is setting the stage for the world community at the end of the age, as predicted in the pages of the Bible.

THE NEW WORLD ORDER

According to God's Word, the end of the age will be characterized by a global government, economy, and religion ruled over by one man, the Antichrist. This end-time world order is described most clearly in Revelation 13.

Global Government

> Authority over every tribe and people and tongue and nation was given to him. (Revelation 13:7b)

Global Religion

> All who dwell on the earth will worship him. (Revelation 13:8a)

Global Economy

> He provides that no one will be able to buy or to sell, except the one who has the mark, either the name of the beast or the number of his name. (Revelation 13:17)

Notice the inclusive, global language that is used in these verses: "every," "all," and "no one." God's Word is clear. A new world order is coming. Globalism is the future.

SATAN: THE MASTER GLOBALIST

Why is there such a push toward globalism? Why is the world being irresistibly drawn together? Is it all a natural result of modern technology, instant communications, worldwide travel, and ubiquitous weapons of mass destruction? Or is there more to it? Is there a hidden power behind all these "modern" developments, pushing a definite agenda?

Many people point to so-called global conspiracies, the trilateral commission, the council on foreign relations, the federal reserve, or the modern-day illuminati as the puppeteers working behind the international scene, pulling the strings. I'm certainly not an expert on conspiracy theories or international economics and politics. But it wouldn't surprise me if they were right, that there *are* powerful, power-hungry men and women with tremendous clout, orchestrating many events to maintain and gain more power.

However, that doesn't mean that they, themselves, aren't under someone else's control. I believe there's an even greater power behind globalism than greedy, influential men. A greater power than mortal mankind. Who or what is this power? I believe that it's Satan himself.

I am convinced that Satan is the driving force behind globalism. Now, in saying this I don't mean that everything about globalism is evil or satanic. What I do mean is that Satan is the impetus behind this movement.

Let me show you why I believe this way.

Satan's original fall into sin was due to his pride. He desired to be like God—to be worshiped as God (see Isaiah 14:12–14; 1 Timothy 3:6). According to Revelation 12:3–4, when Satan led his rebellion, one-third of the angels joined him and followed after him as their newly proclaimed god. In Genesis 3, when Satan appeared in the Garden of Eden in the form of a serpent, he appealed to the man and the woman to trust in *his* word instead of the Word of God. Again, he sought to usurp the place of God.

After the worldwide flood, as the planet became repopulated, the human race was all gathered in one place. According to Genesis 10–11, Nimrod was the human tyrant, or dictator, who led much of the global community—those who did not remain faithful to the Lord. The method these first globalists used to achieve their goal was the building of a city and a tower. They shook their collective fist in God's face and defied His command to scatter over the face of the earth (see Genesis 9:1). They settled down in the land of Shinar at Babel and decided to build a city and a tower to signify and promote their unity.

The city represented their governmental, political

unity, and the tower, or ziggurat, symbolized their religious unity. This ziggurat that reached to the heavens was no doubt intended to be a place of occult worship of the stars and heavens. Therefore, the first federation, or "united nations," was a society built to bring the human race together to exclude God and exalt man—to deify man and dethrone God.

This situation played right into Satan's plan. While he is not mentioned by name in Genesis 10–11, we can be certain that the old serpent introduced in Genesis 3 was working feverishly to energize this rebellion. We can be sure that Satan loved the situation. In this setting he could control, influence, and direct world affairs through one man. And he could be "god" in the eyes of all men, through occult worship and practices.

After all, this is his ultimate desire. Moreover, evil could spread through the whole race with ease since everyone was in one place speaking one language. False religion could also convert the masses with little to stand in its way.

Of course, unknown to all these self-exalted players, God was still in total control. He saw what puny man was doing and He came down and confounded man's language, thus scattering man all over the face of the earth (see Genesis 11:5–8). That was the official end of the first global community.

But Satan wasn't finished. He set out immediately to bring the world back together under his umbrella so he could control it all again.

BACK TO THE FUTURE

Ever since that initial instance of globalism, when Satan ruled the world through one man, Nimrod, it has been Satan's goal to get the world together again so he can rule it all once more. Just think about world history. It's the record of one person after another trying to rule the world. All the power-hungry rulers who have cruelly subjugated nations under their feet have been energized by Satan to foster this great goal of globalization.

Now, for the first time since Genesis 11 and the Tower of Babel, globalization is within man's (and Satan's) reach. Globalization is much more appealing to people today in the post–September 11 world than it was before. All the necessary elements for full-blown, all-out globalization are in place: world travel to almost any place on the planet in a matter of hours, rapid communications, incredible means of surveillance, satellites, weapons of mass destruction that can be used as threats to control others, intertwined world economic markets, the World Bank, etc., etc., etc.

Satan almost has the world back to Babel. All he needs now is one man to bring on the world stage to take over, another Nimrod to rule the world as his puppet. It could happen very soon. The globalism of the last few decades has made this possible for the first time since Genesis 10–11.

THE POINT OF NO RETURN

When I was growing up, I loved watching *Tarzan* on Saturday mornings. It seemed like almost every episode had what I like to call a waterfall scene. Sometime during the show, someone would be in a river, floating along, not realizing that he was being carried toward a deadly waterfall.

The river looked harmless and benign, even peaceful. But it was always deceiving. The person was being pulled by a current that would destroy him. At some point the river reached a point of no return, a place where it was too late to turn back no matter how hard one paddled, swam, or strained. Of course, Tarzan would always come to the rescue just in time, and usually kill a crocodile or two in the process.

The climate of the modern world is very similar.

The current is drawing us farther and farther down the stream of globalism. Closer and closer to the edge. It all seems harmless and benign, even peaceful. But it is leading to the waterfall of destruction, when Antichrist takes control during the Tribulation and uses globalization for his reign of terror, plunging the world into the abyss.

We must remember that the global world of Antichrist cannot suddenly develop in a vacuum. Certain preparations must pave the way. Current events all around us are moving us closer and closer to the edge.

I believe we have already passed the point of no return. The preconditions for globalism are already in place.

Writing in 1965, Billy Graham recognized how world conditions way back then were preparing for Antichrist's global empire.

> There are so many interesting references in the Bible to a future world government to be ruled by a great Antichrist.... It is obvious that the world's acceptance of one-man rule must be preceded by a period of preparation. At a recent peace conference in Washington, speaker after speaker referred

to the necessity and possibility of a world government. In the Gideon Seymour Memorial Lecture at the University of Minnesota, Arnold Toynbee said: "Living together as a single family is the only future mankind can have now that Western technology has simultaneously annihilated distance and invented the atomic bomb." He added: "The alternative to the destruction of the human race is a worldwide social fusion of all the tribes, nations, civilizations, and religions of man."[15]

Make no mistake. Globalism is here to stay and will steadily increase as world organizations take more and more control and become more and more intrusive in national and local governments, and in individual lives. Modern technology will become an ever more powerful tool in the hand of globalists to gain control.

What we see today strikingly portends the global community of the end times that Antichrist will rule over for the last three and a half years of this age.

THE LAST DAYS OF APOSTASY

In 1939, as the Spanish Civil War was drawing to a close, General Mola was making his final plans to attack Madrid. Someone asked him which of his four columns would be the first to enter the city. He responded, "The fifth." His answer became world famous.

General Mola's most important column was a band of rebel sympathizers inside the city. They were already busy at work behind Loyalist lines, aiding his cause. Since that time, the term *fifth column* has been used worldwide to describe traitors who assist the enemy from within.[16]

The Bible uses the word *apostasy* to describe opposition from within. *Apostasy* means "to fall away." It is opposition to the Christian faith from people who profess to believe, who call themselves believers but who believe and teach false doctrine and practice ungodly behavior.

Apostates are consistently characterized by two things in the New Testament: false doctrine and ungodly living. Apostates believe wrong and behave wrong. "They profess to know God, but by their deeds they deny Him" (Titus 1:16).

Apostates are the fifth column within the visible church.

It doesn't take much effort to see that we live in days of surging apostasy. The fifth column is firmly entrenched in almost all the major denominations. More and more churches today are awash in a watered-down, doctrine-less, soft-pedaling, anything-goes, pop psychology, don't-offend-anybody, entertainment-oriented, permissive quagmire.

Or worse yet, many churches actively deny the essential truths of the historic, orthodox faith, such as the virgin birth of Christ, the sinlessness of Christ, the inerrancy of Scripture, the atoning death of Christ for sin, the bodily resurrection of Christ, the necessity of personal faith in Christ for salvation, and the second coming of Christ to earth as King of kings and Lord of lords. For many today, essential doctrine is an unimportant leftover from days gone by. It's seen as divisive and even destructive.

With this wrong belief has come its counterpart—wrong behavior. Sadly, sins that weren't even condoned by the most hardened sinners a generation ago are now being accepted as alternative lifestyles for professing Christians and even ordained ministers.

The most degrading, unnatural vices are no longer called sin, but are even accepted and applauded. Romans 1:24–32 is sometimes called the "stockyards of the New Testament." It describes the low level to which man can sink apart from God. Yet shockingly, individual churches and even entire denominations today are wading knee-deep in the worst kind of moral filth described in this passage of Scripture.

Many of the mainline denominations are already ordaining open, noncelibate homosexuals to the pastorate. Those that have not yet taken this step are actively debating it. What a tragedy! These kinds of issues should never have to be debated. God's Word is crystal clear on the subject. But it seems as if it's just a matter of time until one by one the mainline denominations cave in to the pressure of the new tolerance.

The nature and extent of apostasy today is stagger-ing. As J. Dwight Pentecost, a noted authority on Bible prophecy, says,

> Abundant evidence on every hand shows that men are departing from the faith. Not only do they doubt the Word; they openly reject it. This phenomenon has never been as prevalent as today. In the period of church history known as the dark ages, men were ignorant of the truth; but never was there an age when men openly denied and repudiated the truth. This open, deliberate, willful repudiation of the truth of the Bible is described in Scripture as one of the major characteristics of the last days of the church on earth.[17]

Let's look together at what the New Testament says about the last days of apostasy in the visible church.

FROM BAD TO WORSE

There are a handful of New Testament passages that tell us that apostasy will be one of the defining characteristics of the last days: 1 Timothy 4:1–3; 2 Timothy 3:1–13;

2 Peter 2:1–22; 3:3–6; and Jude 1:1–25. Each of these passages provides important insight into the nature of apostasy in the last days.

First Timothy

First Timothy 4:1 says, "But the Spirit explicitly says that in later times some will fall away from the faith, paying attention to deceitful spirits and doctrines of demons."

The time frame of when this apostasy will occur is defined as the "later times." The word "later," or "latter," indicates that these times were still future when Paul wrote this epistle. The word used here for "times" is the Greek word *kairois*. It refers to seasons, or shorter segments of time. It is plural to indicate that there will be more than one. That is, these times of apostasy will recur intermittently throughout the church age.[18]

Second Timothy

Second Timothy 3:1–5 gives nineteen characteristics of apostasy in the last days.

> But realize this, that in the last days difficult times will come. For men will be lovers of self, lovers of money, boastful, arrogant, revilers, disobedient to

parents, ungrateful, unholy, unloving, irreconcil-able, malicious gossips, without self-control, brutal, haters of good, treacherous, reckless, con-ceited, lovers of pleasure rather than lovers of God, holding to a form of godliness, although they have denied its power; Avoid such men as these.

There are five important keys to understanding this passage of Scripture. *First,* Paul tells Timothy and us to "realize this." To put it in our language, Paul is saying, "Mark this, underline it, highlight it, don't miss it." In other words, this message about apostasy in the last days is something we need to pay full attention to.

Second, what does Paul mean by "the last days"? This is a different expression than the one in 1 Timothy 4:1 ("later times"). Most often in the New Testament, the phrase *last days* relates to the entire time period between the ascension of Christ and His return (see Acts 2:17; Hebrews 1:1–2; 1 Peter 1:20; 1 John 2:18). We often call this period of time the inter-advent age, or the church age.

What Paul is saying in the context of 2 Timothy 3:1 is that during the last days, a period of now almost two thousand years, there will be shorter seasons or periods of time that will be especially difficult, terrible times of apostasy.[19]

The word "difficult" (*chalepos*) in 2 Timothy 3:1 connotes the idea of grievous, or terrible. The only other place this Greek word is found in the New Testament is Matthew 8:28, where the two demoniacs were so *chalepos* that no one could pass by. Plutarch, the famous Greek writer, used this term to describe an ugly, infected wound.

Third, this passage says that while there will be seasons or times of apostasy that are especially terrible within the last days, the overall progression will be for things to worsen. The general progression will be in a downward direction. After the description in 2 Timothy 3:1–5, we are told to expect apostasy to get worse as the church age progresses.

"But evil men and imposters will proceed from bad to worse, deceiving and being deceived" (2 Timothy 3:13). In other words, as this extended period of time known as the last days unfolds, these perilous times of apostasy will become more frequent and intense as the return of Christ nears.

Fourth, we need to recognize that the conditions

described in 2 Timothy 3:1–5 are conditions within the church. Obviously, the kinds of sins listed here have always been prevalent in society at large. The shocking thing here in 2 Timothy 3 is that these sins have now come into the church. Professing Christians are pictured living on the lowest level. The entire context of 2 Timothy 3 is describing people who profess to know God and hold to a form of godliness, yet deny its power.

Fifth, the chief sin of the last-days apostasy, the one that heads the list, is "For men will be lovers of self." Self-love is the polluted fountain from which the other eighteen characteristics flow. It is followed by "lovers of money," and then later comes "lovers of pleasure rather than lovers of God." What a description of the visible church today!

Therefore, what we learn from this passage is that during the last days, there will be times of especially serious, terrible, ugly apostasy in the visible church. And, the overall trend will be for things to proceed from bad to worse. First Timothy 4:1 tells of specific times of apostasy when "some" would be involved. But 2 Timothy 3 goes a step further. It describes a general decadence within the professing church that gets progressively worse. Apostasy will escalate as the church age progresses, reaching its zenith at the end of the age just before Christ returns to rapture to heaven all who have humbly accepted His Son as their Savior from sin.

The escalation of apostasy during this age is setting the stage for the final, ultimate apostasy, which will occur under the Antichrist just before Christ returns to earth (see 2 Thessalonians 2:1–3). In this greatest of all apostasies, men will worship Antichrist as god.

Second Peter

In 2 Peter 2:1–22, the apostle gives a lengthy, scathing diatribe against apostates that he predicted would come into the church to deceive, deny, and disobey the truth.

Second Peter 2:1–2 says, "But false prophets also arose among the people, just as there will also be false teachers among you, who will secretly introduce destructive heresies, even denying the Master who bought them, bringing swift destruction upon themselves. And many will follow their sensuality, and because of them the way of the truth will be maligned."

In 2 Peter 3:3–4, Peter continues, "Know this first of all, that in the last days mockers will come with their mocking, following after their own lusts, and saying, 'Where is the promise of His coming?'"

Peter says apostates even deny the second coming of Christ.

Jude

Jude, the half brother of Jesus, wrote his entire brief epistle (Jude 1:1–25) as a warning that the apostates Peter had warned about a few years earlier had already arrived, worming their way into the church.

It's always been interesting to me that the little epistle of Jude, which is the only book in the Bible devoted exclusively to apostasy, is right before the book of Revelation. It serves as a perfect introduction for Revelation by revealing what the visible, professing church will be like in the days before the events of Revelation are unfolded.

DEPARTING FROM THE FAITH

What we see in the visible church today is nothing short of shocking. I believe we are witnessing the increase and intensification of apostasy we should expect if the coming of Christ is near. While I guess things could always get worse, I find it difficult to believe that things could get much worse than the theological and moral malaise we have witnessed in the last thirty years. Remember, we defined apostasy as wrong belief and wrong behavior by those who profess to know the true God. The Word of God, and godly morality, are being jettisoned and thrown overboard today with impunity. Self-love, love of money, and love of pleasure are not only present in the visible church but also proclaimed from pulpits as the self-help way to true happiness. The motto of the visible church today could be summed up in the words, "Make everyone feel good about themselves." Or, "Don't say anything that will make anyone feel bad." Self-love is the religion of the day.

John Walvoord, in his book *The Church in Prophecy*, observes that what we see today is a sign of the times.

The increment of evil, the growth of hypocrisy, selfishness, and unbelief within the bounds of professing Christendom are according to Scripture signs of the approaching end of the age. Though there are thousands of faithful congregations and many pious souls still bearing a faithful testimony to Christ in our modern day, it is hardly true that the majority of Christendom is bearing a true testimony. It is the exception rather than the rule for the great fundamentals of the church to ring from the pulpit and for the pew to manifest the transforming grace of God in life and sacrificial devotion. In a word, the last days of the church on earth are days of apostasy, theologically and morally, days of unbelief, and days that will culminate in divine judgment.[20]

Walvoord concludes, "In a word, the Scriptures predict that there will be a growing apostasy or departure from the Lord as the church age progresses, and its increase can be understood as a general indication that the Rapture itself is near."[21]

THE UPLOOK

Years ago, during a Bible study, a friend of mine was pointing out the sobering reality of intensifying apostasy in our generation. I have to admit that I found myself getting kind of depressed. It all seemed to be gloom and doom. Then he made this statement, "Remember, the darker the outlook, the brighter the uplook!"

In light of what we have seen in God's Word, I believe that statement is true.

However, let me add this thought. I don't think this means that we should give up and just wait for Jesus to come back while churches fall away all around us. Our Lord left us here with very specific instructions, "Occupy [do business] till I come" (Luke 19:13, KJV). We are responsible to use our talents until the Lord comes. We are to do all we can to spread the good news and stem the tide of apostasy. We don't know when our Lord will come. We must "contend earnestly for the faith which was once for all handed down to the saints" (Jude 1:3).

We are not defeatists. We are the ultimate optimists. Jesus wins!

But the Bible teaches that things must get worse before they get better. And as they do, don't ever forget the uplook. It's always bright.

READING THE SIGNS

I n 2002, Mel Gibson starred in the blockbuster movie *Signs*. Gibson's character was a disillusioned, former Episcopal priest who raises corn on his farm. As the movie begins, he awakens with a start and soon discovers a series of large, intricate crop circles in his cornfield.

At first, he writes the whole thing off as the work of local troublemakers. It means nothing. However, in the next few days these mysterious, unexplainable circles begin to appear all over the world. Television news is dominated by coverage of the phenomenon. What does it mean?

Crop circles had appeared before. But the speed at which they appeared and the quantity of them could not be ignored. It couldn't be a coincidence. It just couldn't be. It had to be a sign. And it was. The signs pointed to a catastrophe of worldwide proportion. The signs signaled an ominous global event.

That's exactly what I see today. All the events in our world today that point toward the scenario of the end times predicted in the Bible cannot be accidental or happenstance. They are happening all over the world, with increasing speed and in greater quantity.

Our world today looks strikingly similar to the one pictured in the Bible in the end times. And the picture continues to develop and become clearer and clearer.

SUMMARIZING THE SEVEN SIGNS

Think about what we have seen in these seven signs:

1. Israel is being regathered to her land after almost two thousand years of exile.
2. Jerusalem is in the world spotlight. She is a burden to all who try to move her.
3. The EU is bringing together the heart of the historical Roman Empire.
4. The Middle East peace process is the number one international issue.
5. Iraq, the country of ancient Babylon, has risen to world prominence.

6. Globalism is rapidly replacing nationalism as the new world order.
7. The growing apostasy of the visible church is surging all around us.

If I were trying to write a script to pave the way for the events described in the Bible for the end times, it would be impossible for me to improve on the developing scenario in the world right now. Events all around us fit remarkably into the framework of prophecy predicted for the end of the age. I can't think of any major stage-setting event for the end times that is not currently taking shape.

Realistically, one has to ask, "How long can these conditions persist before the top blows off?" People might say, "Well, times have been difficult at other periods in world history."

But I believe it's different today for two simple reasons. First, what happens in one part of the world is no longer contained. We immediately know what's happening all over the world. And what happens in one place has almost instant impact everywhere else. There's an exponential acceleration in the expansion and effect of events in our world today. How long can fanatics be denied access to weapons of mass destruction? How much longer can the continuous buildup of world tension be restrained? The world seems headed downhill toward a cataclysmic crisis. That crisis could very well be the coming Tribulation, climaxed by Armageddon.

Second, we have never seen all these signs come together like this at any other time. Israel, scattered for almost two thousand years, is returning. The Roman Empire, fractured for almost 1,600 years, is coming back together. Babylon, which disappeared from history as a great empire 2,500 years ago, is back in the picture. Globalism picks up speed every day. Jerusalem, the Middle East, and the ongoing peace process dominate world news every day. And the visible church is turning away from the truth and biblical morality with breathtaking speed.

I believe this is a very unique time that points toward the events of the end. Coming events are casting their shadows ahead of them.

But sadly, most people today are totally unaware of what's happening. In his great book *World Aflame*, Billy Graham described the complacency of our times.

In a declining culture, one of it characteristics is that ordinary people are unaware of what is happening. Only those who know and read the signs of decadence are posing the questions that as yet have no answer. Mr. Average Man is comfortable in his complacency and is unconcerned as a silverfish in a carton of discarded magazines on world affairs. He is not asking any questions because his social benefits from the government give him a false sense of security. This is his trouble and his tragedy. Modern man has become a spectator of world events, observing on his television screen without becoming involved. He watches ominous events of our times pass before his eyes while he sips his beer in a comfortable chair. He does not seem to realize what is happening to him. He does not understand that his world is on fire, and he is about to burned up with it.[22]

In stark contrast, there are those who are ready for the coming of Christ. There are those who know and read the signs of ominous events in our world today and turn to Jesus Christ for salvation.

"BRIDGE OUT"

I heard a story recently about two pastors standing near the side of a road holding up a sign that read, "The end is near! Turn yourself around now before it's too late!"

As the first driver sped by, he hollered, "Leave us alone, you religious nuts!"

From around the curve they heard screeching tires and a big crash.

One pastor turned to the other and said, "Maybe we should just put up a sign that says, 'Bridge Out' instead?"

It does appear to me, as I read the signs in our world today, that the "bridge is out."

So what should you do if the bridge is out? The advice of the preacher with the sign is pretty good. "Turn around now before it's too late."

If you have never personally received Jesus Christ as your Savior from sin, you need to turn around right now and go the opposite direction by turning to Christ for salvation. All who refuse His gracious, free offer of salvation will end in a big crash. The biggest crash of all.

The signs are all around you. The Rapture may occur very soon. Even today. Don't be left behind to crash in the Tribulation and spend eternity in hell. Turn around right now! You can turn around by praying a simple prayer like this:

> *Lord, I know that I'm a sinner and that I desperately*
> *need You. I know that I cannot save myself. I must*
> *have a Savior. And I know that Jesus is the Savior I*
> *need. I receive Him now as my Savior and my Lord.*
> *I confess that He is God and that He died and rose*
> *again for me. Thank You, Lord, for saving me.*
> *Empower and energize me by Your Spirit to live for*
> *You until You come again. Amen.*

If you have prayed that prayer, find a loving, Bible-teaching church where you can serve and be served. Go talk to the pastor of the church about being baptized. Begin to regularly read and study your Bible. Pray to your heavenly Father every day. Witness for Christ both by your works and your words.

And keep looking up.

Jesus may come today!

Multnomah Publishers®
The publisher and author would love to hear your com-
ments about this book. *Please contact us at:*
www.multnomah.net/hitchcock

NOTES

1. Nancy Gibbs, "The Bible and the Apocalypse," *Time,* 1 July 2002, 40–48.
2. Arnold Fruchtenbaum, *The Footsteps of the Messiah* (Tustin, Calif.: Ariel Ministries Press, 1983), 65.
3. Ibid., 67.
4. Randall Price, *Jerusalem in Prophecy: God's Final Stage for the Final Drama* (Eugene, Ore.: Harvest House Publishers, 1998), 219.
5. Fruchtenbaum, *The Footsteps of the Messiah,* 68.
6. John F. Walvoord, *Prophecy in the New Millennium: A Fresh Look at Future Events* (Grand Rapids, Mich.: Kregel Publications, 2001), 61–62.
7. Price, *Jerusalem in Prophecy,* 220.

8. Thomas Ice and Timothy Demy, *The Truth About Jerusalem in Bible Prophecy* (Eugene, Ore.: Harvest House Publishers, 1996), 8.

9. Walvoord, *Prophecy in the New Millennium,* 14.

10. Ibid., 15.

11. Thomas Ice and Timothy Demy, *The Truth About the Signs of the Times* (Eugene, Ore.: Harvest House Publishers, 1997), 37.

12. Charles Dyer, *The Rise of Babylon* (Wheaton, Ill.: Tyndale House Publishers, 1991), 57–65.

13. *Webster's New Collegiate Dictionary* (Springfield, Mass.: G. & C. Merriam Company, 1973), 81.

14. Charles Dyer, "Babylon: Iraq and the Coming Middle East Crisis," in *The Road to Armageddon* (Nashville: Word Publishing, 1999), 136–37.

15. Billy Graham, *World Aflame* (Old Tappan, N.J.: Fleming Revell Company, 1965), 193.

16. George Sweeting, "Betrayal in the Church," *Moody,* April 1992, 74.

17. J. Dwight Pentecost, *Will Man Survive?* (Grand Rapids, Mich.: Zondervan Publishing House, 1980), 58.

18. Homer A. Kent, Jr., *The Pastoral Epistles* (Chicago: Moody Press, 1986), 143.

19. Ibid., 272.
20. John F. Walvoord, *The Church in Prophecy* (Grand Rapids, Mich.: Zondervan Publishing House, 1964), 66.
21. Ibid., 50.
22. Billy Graham, *World Aflame,* 13–14.

END TIMES ANSWERS

WHAT ON EARTH IS GOING ON?

Pierce through the post-9/11 clouds of sensationalism and skepticism with prophecy expert Mark Hitchcock, as he gives a balanced view of today's major global developments signaling Christ's return.

ISBN 1-57673-853-1

IS AMERICA IN BIBLE PROPHECY?

Will America suffer a great fall? Find out what's in store for the world's superpower in the coming days, with prophecy scholar and pastor Mark Hitchcock.

ISBN 1-57673-496-X

THE COMING ISLAMIC INVASION OF ISRAEL

Mark Hitchcock shows how events today may be setting the stage for the fulfillment of Ezekiel's prediction—a Russian-Islamic confederation of nations will finally invade Israel and be destroyed by God.

ISBN 1-59052-048-3

IS THE ANTICHRIST ALIVE TODAY?

Is there an Antichrist alive today, right now, in this generation? Prophecy expert Mark Hitchcock discusses five events today preparing the world for the Antichrist's reign.

ISBN 1-59052-075-0

"The End Is Near!"

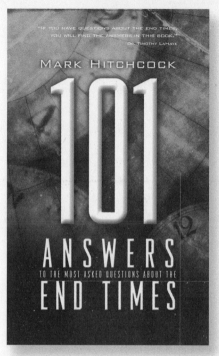

"Mark's book fills a real need in the study of prophecy. Finally, there's one book that gives solid, biblical answers to all the key questions that people today are asking about the end times."

—DR. TIMOTHY LAHAYE

Or is it? The Antichrist is alive and well today! *Or is he?* The church is about to be raptured and will certainly escape the Tribulation…*right?* When it comes to the end times, there's so much confusion. Preachers with elaborate charts share their theories about Revelation and other prophetic books of the Bible. "Ah, Babylon stands for the United States," they say. But then other teachers share their theories: "No, Babylon stands for the Roman Catholic Church, or the European Union, or the literal Babylon rebuilt in Iraq…." *Would somebody please shoot straight with me?* Finally, someone has. Gifted scholar and pastor Mark Hitchcock walks you gently through Bible prophecy in an engaging, user-friendly style. Hitchcock's careful examination of the topic will leave you feeling informed and balanced in your understanding of events to come…in our time?

ISBN 1-57673-952-X